LUTON LIBRARI

Renewals, online accounts, catalogue searches,
eBooks and other online services:

https://arena.yourlondonlibrary.net/web/luton/

Renewals: 01582 547413, (24hr) 0333 370 4700

Illus ————————————————————— t

Japc

**Luton
Culture**

Edited by Jenny Tyler and Mairi Mackinnon

Designed by Mike Olley and Holly Lamont

9 22000000 89 928

 There is a little yellow duck to find in every picture.

いま　*ima*　The living room

おとうさん
otōsan　Daddy

おかあさん
okāsan　Mummy

おとこのこ
otoko no ko　boy

2

おんなのこ
onna no ko girl

あかちゃん
akachan baby

いぬ
inu dog

ねこ
neko cat

ようふく

yōfuku   Clothes

くつ

kutsu   shoes

パンツ

pantsu   pants

セーター

sētā   jumper

ランニングシャツ　ズボン　Ｔシャツ　ソックス
ranningu-shatsu　vest　*zubon*　trousers　*tīshatsu*　t-shirt　*sokkusu*　socks

あさごはん

 *asagohan*　**Breakfast**

パン
pan　bread

ぎゅうにゅう
gyūnyū　milk

たまご
tamago　eggs

りんご
ringo   apple

オレンジ
orenji   orange

バナナ
banana   banana

だいどころ

 *daidokoro* The kitchen

テーブル
tēburu table

いす
isu chair

おさら
o-sara plate

8

ナイフ
naifu　knife

フォーク
fōku　fork

スプーン
supūn　spoon

カップ
kappu　cup

9

おもちゃ　*omocha*　Toys

うま
uma　horse

ひつじ
hitsuji　sheep

うし
ushi　cow

にわとり
niwatori   hen

ぶた
buta   pig

きしゃ
kisha   train

つみき
tsumiki   bricks

ほうもん

hōmon   On a visit

おばあさん
obāsan   Granny

おじいさん
ojīsan   Grandpa

しつないばき
shitsunaibaki   slippers

コート
kōto coat

ワンピース
wanpiisu dress

ぼうし
bōshi hat

こうえん
kōen　**The park**

き
ki　tree

はな
hana　flower

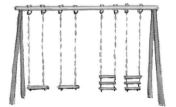
ブランコ
buranko　swings

ボール
bōru　ball

すべりだい
suberidai   slide

ながぐつ
nagagutsu   boots

とり
tori   bird

ふね
fune   boat

とおり

tōri   **The street**

くるま
kuruma   car

じてんしゃ
jitensha   bicycle

ひこうき
hikōki   plane

16

トラック
torakku   truck

バス
basu   bus

いえ
ie   house

パーティー

 pātī The party

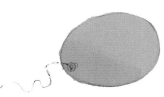

ふうせん
fūsen balloon

ケーキ
kēki cake

とけい
tokei clock

アイスクリーム
aisu kuriimu   ice cream

さかな
sakana   fish

ビスケット
bisuketto   biscuits

おかし
o-kashi   sweets

プール

pūru　　The swimming pool

うで
ude　arm

て
te　hand

あし
ashi　leg

あし
ashi feet

つまさき
tsumasaki toes

あたま
atama head

おしり
o-shiri bottom

こういしつ

kōishitsu　　The changing room

くち

kuchi　mouth

め

me　eyes

みみ

mimi　ears

はな
hana　nose

かみ
kami　hair

くし
kushi　comb

ブラシ
burashi　brush

おみせ　*o-mise*　The shop

あか
aka　red

あお
ao　blue

みどり
midori　green

24

きいろ
ki-iro　yellow

ピンク
pinku　pink

しろ
shiro　white

くろ
kuro　black

よくしつ

yokushitsu **The bathroom**

せっけん
sekken soap

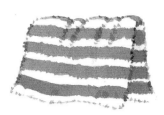

タオル
taoru towel

トイレ
toire toilet

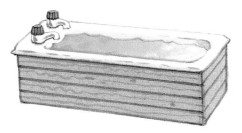

おふろ
ofuro   bath

おなか
onaka   tummy

あひる
ahiru   duck

しんしつ

shinshitsu **The bedroom**

ベッド
beddo bed

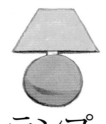

ランプ
ranpu lamp

まど
mado window

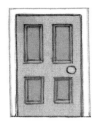
ドア
doa   door

ほん
hon   book

にんぎょう
ningyō   doll

テディベア
tedībea   teddy bear

Match the words to the pictures

アイスクリーム	りんご	ランプ	ランニングシャツ
aisu kuriimu	*ringo*	*ranpu*	*ranningu-shatsu*

あひる
ahiru

いぬ
inu

うし
ushi

オレンジ
orenji

きしゃ
kisha

くるま
kuruma

ケーキ
kēki

ぎゅうにゅう	さかな	セーター	ソックス
gyūnyū	*sakana*	*sētā*	*sokkusu*

まど
mado

ボール
bōru

ぼうし
bōshi

ベッド
beddo

バナナ
banana

ほん
hon

フォーク
fōku

ねこ
neko

にんぎょう
ningyō

ながぐつ
nagagutsu

ナイフ
naifu

たまご
tamago

テーブル
tēburu

テディベア
tedībea

とけい
tokei

かず *kazu* Numbers

1 いち
ichi one

2 に
ni two

3 さん
san three

4 し
shi four

5 ご
go five

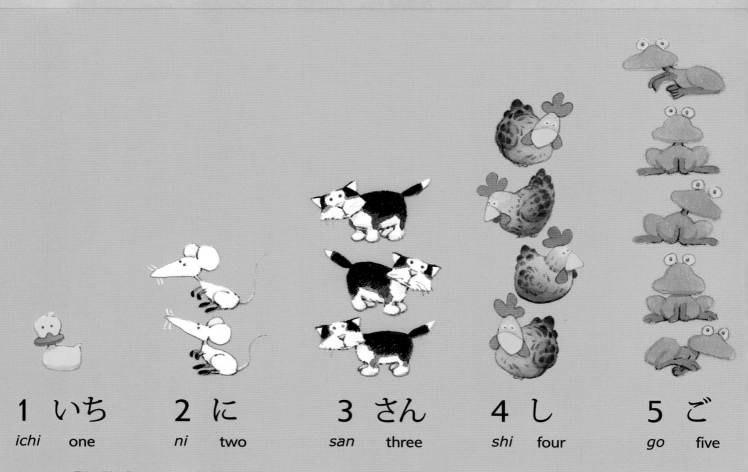

1 いち
ichi one

2 に
ni two

3 さん
san three

4 し
shi four

5 ご
go five